# JavaScript for Beginners

# Table Of Contents

Preface ............................................................. 1

Chapter 1: Introduction to JavaScript ................ 4

   JavaScript as a Client-Side Scripting Language ........................................................ 4

      NOTE ......................................................... 5

      FYI ............................................................. 6

   JavaScript as the Web's Assembly Language . 6

      NOTE ......................................................... 6

      FYI ............................................................. 7

   JavaScript as a Programming Language ........ 8

Chapter 2: Introduction to Programming and Scripting ............................................................. 9

   What Is A Program? ......................................... 9

   How Do Programs Work and How Do Computers Execute Them? ............................. 9

   How to Create a Program ............................. 10

   What Is A Programming Language? .............. 10

   Scripts and Programs — How Are They Different? ........................................................ 11

   Scripts ............................................................ 12

Chapter 3: Purposes of JavaScript ...................... 13
    FYI ............................................................. 14
  What Can JavaScript Do? ............................... 15
    NOTE ......................................................... 15

Chapter 4: Embedding JavaScript in Your HTML Files ......................................................... 17
  JavaScript Placing: Internal Coding ............... 17
    NOTE ......................................................... 18
    NOTE ......................................................... 20
    NOTE ......................................................... 20
  JavaScript Placing: External Linking .............. 21
    NOTE ......................................................... 21
    FYI ............................................................. 22

Chapter 5: JavaScript Syntax ............................. 23
  How Is JavaScript Read? ................................ 24
  White Space ................................................... 26
  Physical Line and Logical Line ....................... 26
  Physical Line Length ...................................... 26
  Line Breaks .................................................... 27
    TIP ............................................................. 28
  Case Sensitivity .............................................. 29
  Camel Casing ................................................. 29

## Chapter 6: Statement and Its Parts ............... 31
- NOTE ............................................................. 32
- TIP ................................................................. 33
- Literals ............................................................. 33
- Variables ......................................................... 35
  - TIP ............................................................. 36
  - TIP ............................................................. 37
  - TIP ............................................................. 37
  - NOTE ......................................................... 38
  - NOTE ......................................................... 38
- Identifiers ....................................................... 38
  - TIP ............................................................. 39
- Operators ........................................................ 40
  - NOTE ......................................................... 41
- Assignment Operator ..................................... 42
- Expressions .................................................... 43
  - NOTE ......................................................... 44
- Keywords ........................................................ 45
- Comments ...................................................... 45

## Chapter 7: Code Blocks and Functions ........ 49
- JavaScript Function ....................................... 50
- Invoking Functions in JavaScript .................. 52
- Alert ................................................................ 53

    Function Parameters ........................................ 54

Chapter 8: Conditional Statements .................... 56
    If Conditional Statement ................................. 56
    If Else Conditional Statement ........................ 58
    Else If Statement ............................................. 60
    Applications ..................................................... 62
Conclusion ............................................................ 63

# Copyright

JavaScript For Beginners

Written By Adam Vardy

Copyright © 2015
All rights reserved.

This book or any portion thereof may not be reproduced or used in any manner whatsoever without the expressed written permission of the publisher except for the use of brief quotation in a book review.

# Preface

This book will teach you the basics of JavaScript and will prepare you for more intermediate aspects of this client-side scripting language. The lessons that will be provided will focus on the applications of JavaScript on web development — primarily, on how you can use it with HTML and CSS.

If you are a complete beginner in programming, the book will serve as an introduction to programming. Most of the ideas that you will learn here can be used and referenced when you decide to learn another language — whether it is scripting or multipurpose programming language.

On the other hand, take note that you must have at least basic understanding of HTML before learning JavaScript. It is a prerequisite that you must accomplish. Knowledge in CSS is optional, but it is also recommended that you learn it, too, before learning JavaScript.

Additionally, the chapters will be peppered with examples. Most of them will be explained bit by bit. However, it is recommended that you analyze the codes first before you read the explanations. Try to understand them without relying too much on the succeeding details that explain what those codes do. It is good practice.

After getting used to it, reading a code and understanding its context without any explanation is a good skill that you can take advantage of once you decide to earn money coding JavaScript or programming.

Just like with coding HTML, the only tools you need to develop JavaScript codes or scripts is a regular text editing program and a web browser. However, it is also advisable that you get and use a decent source code editor instead of a regular text editor.

The additional features of source code editors, such as syntax highlighting and folding, will make script development easier and faster. But if you want to do it the hard way and 'hardcode' the things you will learn in here in your head, then text editors are the way to go.

Another thing: The book will also be peppered with FYIs, notes, and tips. FYIs will just give you some good-to-know information. They can be helpful if you are serious in advancing your knowledge in computer programming and JavaScript scripting. But if you just want to get a bit familiar with JavaScript, then you can skip them.

Alternatively, notes are there to provide information about crucial things that you must retain in your mind. They will also serve as reminders. And tips are pretty self-explanatory, don't you think?

You can learn how to do JavaScript in your web pages in a week or two. Spend at least four to six hours reading and applying the things written here, and you will be able to pick almost everything up.

Some who are good at logic and math will have an easy time learning this client-side scripting language. Alternatively, those who have a background in programming can just read this book like a reviewer or a basic reference to programming and scripting.

If ever you find yourself having a hard time understanding the materials in this book, take a break or have fun using the things you have just learned. It is common that new programmers or even veteran ones will be stuck at some point when programming. And the usual culprit is mental fatigue. Staying away from the computer for a few minutes to an hour can help on getting you back on track.

Good luck.

# Chapter 1: Introduction to JavaScript

JavaScript is a programming or scripting language most commonly used in websites. It is usually used in conjunction with HTML (HTML5), CSS (CSS3), Ajax, PHP, and MySQL in order to provide web surfers with rich and dynamic websites or web pages.

Alternatively, JavaScript allows the developer to have greater control of the pages that his website displays to its visitors — for example, disabling the right click context menu and preventing visitors to view the pages' source codes.

## JavaScript as a Client-Side Scripting Language

JavaScript is also referred as a client-side scripting (not to be confused with CSS, which means Cascaded Style Sheet) language. As its name implies, client-side scripting roughly means that the programs or instructions written on the script are only run or executed in the client's machine or software.

In the Web, a web page visitor is considered as a client; the server or website that supplements the web pages is considered as the server; and the browser and computer that the client uses is considered as the client machine and browser. In some cases, the computer or browser is referred to as the client.

A few of the most common and popular client-side scripting languages used in the Web are ActionScript, VBScript, Dart, TypeScript, and Python. A few of those scripting languages are also capable of being server-side scripting languages, such as JavaScript, Python, and VBScript.

A client-side script allows regular Web or static HTML pages to become dynamic or become a Dynamic HTML page. In layman's terms, such scripts that are written and embedded in web pages allow those pages to have dynamic content, become feature-rich, and be capable of simple or even advanced interactions or responses toward the user or web page viewer's actions.

> ***NOTE***
> *JavaScript is different from the Java programming language. Technically, JavaScript is ECMA Script. However, JavaScript was the one chosen to be used to be the language's trademark name.*
>
> *On the other hand, the two have similarities. The most pronounced similarity of the two is their syntax, which is also relatively similar to the popular languages such as C, C++, and C#. Also, JavaScript developers and JavaScript itself loosely follow the coding style standards of Java and Java developers.*

> **FYI**
> *Static pages are HTML files that do not contain any scripts or calls that can allow themselves to command the browser that views them to do something except from displaying the page only.*
>
> *Also, client-side scripting is not the only thing that makes static pages dynamic. Server-side scripts written in server-side scripting languages such as PHP, ASP, Java, Python, Ruby, et cetera, are also capable of creating dynamic web pages.*

## JavaScript as the Web's Assembly Language

Many web developers regard JavaScript as one of the biggest components of the Web — to the point that they consider it as the Web's assembly language. If it disappears suddenly from the face of the Internet, chaos will ensue.

A lot of websites will not work, security vulnerabilities will happen, and web developers will panic to death. After all, JavaScript will not be the only one affected. Ajax (asynchronous JavaScript and XML) will be affected, too.

> **NOTE**
> *Ajax will be covered later, but for you to have an idea what it is, Ajax is a web development technique that allows some core web page actions or events possible*

*without the browser refreshing or redirecting the page being viewed. A good example that uses Ajax is a typical chat application in a website.*

***FYI***
*On the other hand, assembly language is relatively the same with machine language. In programming, assembly language is considered as the rawest form of programming languages and all programs written in modern programming languages are translated to assembly in order for the computer to understand the written instructions.*

*In this case, JavaScript is considered as the assembly language of the Web because most modern browsers can inherently understand JavaScript in its rawest form. Some of the client-side scripting languages that treat JavaScript as an 'assembly language' are JSON and jQuery.*

Nevertheless, it does not mean that the disappearance of JavaScript on the Web will be the end of the Internet. It will just mean that a lot of problems will occur. And most online business will be hampered or devastated.

# JavaScript as a Programming Language

Essentially, JavaScript is a programming language. A programming language is a tool that can allow humans to communicate and tell computers what they want to do. After all, programming in its basic form is an action that makes computers perform the things you want to do by writing sequences of computer instructions.

It has been said a lot before that JavaScript is a popular scripting language for web developers. Primarily, JavaScript garners this kind of attention because it is easy to learn. Even without any programming experience or knowledge, JavaScript can be learned. It can also serve as a good introductory language for those who want to become programmers — either for Web, for computers, or for mobile devices.

# Chapter 2: Introduction to Programming and Scripting

This chapter will teach you the basics of programming. As a disclaimer, some explanations on this chapter are crude and oversimplified. They are intended for the purpose of just giving you an idea and letting you see the big picture. For most, this might be good-to-know information only. However, for newbies, it is encouraged that they need to know all of these details.

## What Is A Program?

A program is a file that contains instructions that the computer must execute.

## How Do Programs Work and How Do Computers Execute Them?

Typically, the computer will load the program first on its memory or RAM. Depending on the computer, operating system, or the program itself, the loading process might be different. Nevertheless, the loading process is a crucial step in executing programs. When the program is loaded or 'copied' to the memory, the processor will start executing the instructions written on it.

Why does the computer need to load the program in the memory anyway? It is already present in the storage device (hard disk drive,

USB disk drive, et cetera), right? Primarily, programs are loaded into the memory for faster execution. RAM 'sticks' provide faster read and write speeds compared to other data storage devices such as hard disk drives, USB sticks, and optical storage devices (CD and DVD).

Also, depending on the program, the processor might need to reread the program's contents or instructions repeatedly and write the sets of data that the program will create during execution. And again, speed is important. If the processor relies on a slower storage media device, execution will take long amounts of time, especially if the program is huge.

## How to Create a Program

To create a program, you must write its source code using a programming language. The source code will contain lines of instructions that you want the computer to perform. Each instruction is called a statement. A statement can be composed of multiple tokens or elements. These elements can be variables, operators, expressions, keywords, et cetera; they will be discussed later.

## What Is A Programming Language?

Once you think that your source code is complete or it can be the program that you want to run, the next step is to translate it into a language that a computer can understand — for it to become capable of performing the instructions that you have written.

Why does it need to be translated? Computers understand programming language by default, right? No. The only language that the computer can understand is machine or binary language. To some extent, computers can understand assembly language.

A programming language is a set of development tools designed to allow people create programs and send instructions to computers. It bridges the language barrier between humans and computers. Due to the limitation of the computer to understand only one language, which humans cannot easily comprehend, most programming languages rely on compilers and interpreters.

A programming language contains interpreters, compilers, libraries, and the language itself. Compilers and interpreters roughly perform the translation needed by the computer to understand your source code. And this is where the separation of scripts and compiled programs comes in.

## Scripts and Programs — How Are They Different?

To simplify matters, programs are fully translated source codes and scripts are source codes that are only translated when they are used. Programs use compilers and scripts use interpreters. However, either one may use both or other tools to become a functional program.

An example of a compiled program is Microsoft Window's Notepad. An example of a script is a JavaScript script in a web page. However, they are both considered software.

Unlike a regular JavaScript script, you cannot edit the source code of a compiled or fully translated program like Notepad since it is already translated to machine/assembly language, which can be unreadable anymore to new and regular programmers.

## Scripts

As mentioned a while ago, a script is often left as a source code. It will be only translated when it is used. Its biggest advantage is that you can edit it anytime.

However, in order for a script to run or let the computer understand the instructions you wrote, it will need an interpreter or a translator. In JavaScript, browsers act as the interpreter, so you do not need to worry about that.

## Chapter 3: Purposes of JavaScript

You have now an idea on what JavaScript is and a bit of how programming works. In this chapter, you will be familiarized on what it can actually do and what you can do with it.

By the way, you should remember that if you are an aspiring web developer or website owner, you need to master three languages. They are:

1. HTML: Hypertext Markup Language is what you use to tell browsers what content will be shown and how your content will be displayed. You use it to define the elements that will be present on your pages and the contents that will be inside those elements.
2. CSS: Cascading Style Sheet is what you use to tell browsers how your elements and contents will be laid out on your visitor's screen. It can be also done with HTML alone, but it is much easier to do with CSS.
3. JS: JavaScript is what you use to control HTML and CSS before, during, and after the browser reads and renders the HTML and CSS codes embedded on your page. You will use it to improve and add functionalities to your web page.

***FYI***

*In case that you want to become an advanced web developer, you need to learn two more types of languages (or systems). And they are:*

1. *Server-side scripting language: The most popular one you can learn is PHP (Hypertext Preprocessor). Primarily, server-side scripting languages are used to provide dynamic content. Aside from that, they are usually used to provide Software as Service (SaaS) on the Web. You can use them to manage your server's database, too.*

2. *Database Management System: The most popular one you can learn is MySQL. You use database in your servers to store information about your site, users, or anything you find relevant.*

    *For example, you use a database management system to store your user's usernames, passwords, and even emails. On the other hand, you can use it to store your content, file, and other important data for your website. DBMS and server-side scripting language often go hand in hand.*

*On the other hand, if you want to become a full stack developer or web server administrator, you will need to learn operating systems, networking, and HTTP servers aside from those that were previously mentioned. The most commonly used OS for servers is Linux. The most commonly used HTTP server program is Apache.*

## What Can JavaScript Do?

Primarily, JavaScript can be used to change or update an HTML element's content. You can do that by writing a single line of code. For example:

document.getElementById("testElement").innerHTML = "New Content";


In that example, the script assigns a new value to the innerHTML property of the HTML element that has an id attribute of 'testElement'. If the browser executes that code in an HTML page with a paragraph element with an id of 'testElement', its content will be changed into 'New Content'.

> ***NOTE***
>
> *As of now, the purpose of these examples and explanations is to familiarize you with JavaScript. The book will discuss most of the things that will be mentioned here in detail later.*

Aside from that, JavaScript can also allow you to change the value of an element's attribute. The process is almost the same as the previous one. For example:

document.getElementById("testImage").src = "/differentImage.jpg";

Aside from manipulating regular HTML values, you can use JavaScript to alter CSS-related attributes. In this case, you will need to access the element's style attribute and provide the value that you want to assign to the style property that you want to change. For example:

document.getElementById("testElement").style.fontSize = "16px";

And those are only a few of the things that JavaScript can do to your web pages. The other things that it can do are:

- Generate pop-up boxes
- Analyze the content of the elements
- Perform arithmetic operations
- Animate elements using CSS
- Remove, add, and change elements present in the web page

# Chapter 4: Embedding JavaScript in Your HTML Files

JavaScript scripts are usually embedded in HTML files. JavaScript codes, just like any client-side scripting language codes, are placed inside HTML script tags: <script> and </script>.

## JavaScript Placing: Internal Coding

Unlike other HTML tags that should be placed in the <head> tag in an HTML file, the <script> tag containing a JavaScript code can be placed anywhere in an HTML document. To be precise, you can place JavaScript codes in the <body> and/or <head> sections of an HTML file. For example:

```
<!DOCTYPE html>
<html>
<head>
 <title>Example Page</title>
 <script>
  alert("sample message");
 </script>
</head>
<body>
 <h1>Sample Header</h1>
 <p>Sample paragraph.</p>
</body>
</html>
```

> **NOTE**
>
> *In older versions of browsers or JavaScript, you must indicate the type attribute in your script tag when inserting JavaScript code. In that case, you will need to indicate the value: "text/javascript".*
>
> *For example:*
>
> *<script type = "text/javascript">*
>
> *... example code goes here ...*
>
> *</script>*
>
> *However, newer versions of browsers (or modern browsers in general) do not require you to declare the type of script that you will insert in the script tag if you are going to use JavaScript. Modern browsers recognize or expect that any script that you place in the script tag is a JavaScript code.*

In the example, the JavaScript code was placed inside the head section of the HTML document. And it is standard practice that most of the scripts in your web pages should be in the head section. However, you might want to place your JavaScript codes somewhere else in some cases.

Take note that the location of your JavaScript codes affects the time when they will be read and executed. The JavaScript line or statement in the example will instruct the browser to launch a message or pop-up box that will contain the message 'sample message'.

You might want to try copying the example and saving it as an HTML file. After that, try opening the HTML file using any web browser that you prefer. Once you do that, did you notice anything?

Just after you access the page, the message box will immediately appear on your browser. Despite the page being still blank, the browser has already processed the script. The reason is that browsers parse and execute your HTML file line per line. And since the JavaScript code is on the head section, it will be read first before the body of your HTML file.

What does that mean? It means that before your browser renders the visible parts of your page, which usually are confined inside the body section of HTML files, the browser will immediately execute the JavaScript file.

On the other hand, if you place the JavaScript at the end of the body section — or just way past the heading and paragraph elements, the browser will render the two elements first on the display and then launch the message box.

Alternatively, if you place the JavaScript code between the heading element and paragraph element, what will happen is that the browser will render the heading first, launch the message box, and then render the paragraph element last.

***NOTE***
*When alert or message boxes are launched in the browser, the page where the pop-up boxes originated from will be paused until the user closes the message box. In most cases, alert boxes are used for debugging purposes due to the behavior that it enforces to the browser. These things will be discussed in more detail later.*

***NOTE***
*As good practice, it is best that you make sure that you place all of your JavaScript codes in one place only. It enforces a neater and clutter-free HTML file. Also, doing it that way makes your JavaScripts easier to debug later. In most cases, JavaScripts are placed inside the head tag or section. After all, the head section is usually dedicated to non-visible elements, meta descriptions, styling rules, and scripting codes.*

*On the other hand, it does not mean that placing your scripts in the body section of your web pages is a bad thing. Most commonly, web developers tend to place their huge JavaScripts at the bottom of their pages' body section.*

*The rationale behind that is placing huge scripts at the last part of the body section implicitly tells the browser to render the page first before the scripts — doing so increases page load performance, display-wise.*

## JavaScript Placing: External Linking

Aside from inserting your JavaScript code within your HTML file, you can save them in a file and then link them to your page — just like when you link external CSS sheets. For example:

```
<!DOCTYPE html>
<html>
<head>
 <title>Example Page</title>
 <script src = "sampleExternalScript.js" >
</script>
</head>
<body>
 <h1>Sample Header</h1>
 <p>Sample paragraph.</p>
</body>
</html>
```

> ***NOTE***
>
> *When creating an external JavaScript file, make sure that you do not include the script tags anymore. Just like with CSS, everything that is placed in the linked file will be placed in between the tags 'virtually'.*
>
> *On the other hand, JavaScript files use the file extension .js.*

Using external JavaScript files are useful in case you plan to reuse some lines of codes in multiple pages. Also, the external JavaScript codes allow you to write HTML documents with less clutter since it effectively separates your JavaScript codes and HTML — the same way you separate CSS rules and HTML.

Aside from that, once the JavaScript is cached in the client's browser, page loading can become faster. It also lightens your server's load and lessens the need of the client to download and download the codes again.

> ***FYI***
> *External linking will allow you to use open-source JavaScript libraries such as MooTools, Prototype, and jQuery. These libraries or frameworks can provide you with added functionalities in your JavaScript code. Some can make your coding life easier. Nevertheless, you need to be concerned about these libraries in the future if you want to advance your JavaScript mastery further.*

## Chapter 5: JavaScript Syntax

In this section, you will start understanding how to write or program JavaScript code. And as a standard when learning programming language, you will start learning about this scripting language's syntax.

A syntax is a set of rules that you need to follow when writing codes. It is very much similar to grammar. And technically, it is safe to say that syntax is the grammar of a programming language.

However, unlike the English grammar, a programming language's syntax is stricter but simpler. The strictness and simplicity of the syntax depend on the programming language. Compared to most programming languages, JavaScript is in the middle of things.

Syntax rules are strict because one simple mistake in your source code might lead to unintended effects that you do not want. Computer programs require precision and great care. And despite being strict, syntax is simpler. This is to prevent any complications in the instructions. After all, unlike humans, computers cannot understand context.

Computers are 'simple' machines that will do anything that you say as long as your instruction makes sense for them, even if it does not make sense to you – or if your instruction incidentally becomes erroneous or against what you want due to typos or other human-related errors.

By the way, if you try to run your script that is filled with syntax errors, a few of these things might happen:

- The script will do a different thing than you intended.
- The script will not work.
- The browser executing the script might crash.
- The page might not render properly at all.
- The browser might inform you about the errors.

## How Is JavaScript Read?

Just like a regular program, the statements within a JavaScript code are executed one by one, according to their order in the document. The browser will start reading and executing statements at the topmost part of the document. For example:

```
<script>
 var someVariable;
 someVariable = 2;
</script>
```

The browser will first define the variable someVariable and then assign the numerical literal 2 to it. Check this next example:

```
<script>
 someVariable = 2;

  var someVariable;
</script>
```

In this case, the assignment came first on top. Even if it is logical to execute the definition of the variable first, the browser will still try to execute the assignment since it is found on the first line of the script.

Anyway, the browser does not immediately execute a code. First, it will read the statement first. After that, it will check if the statement is valid by checking if the statement followed the syntax. In case that there is an error, the browser will stop processing the script. If the statement is okay, then the browser will execute it, and move on to the next one.

So, in the previous example, the script will not push through since the script tried to assign a value to a variable that was not yet defined.

Some browsers try to ignore erroneous lines. Some of them even have a function that corrects some of some simple syntax errors while some are lenient. Nevertheless, it is not a good enough reason to slack off when it comes to debugging and cleaning your scripts.

## White Space

Just like in HTML, browsers ignore multiple or trailing spaces in your JavaScript code. In some cases, you can get away with not using spaces. However, it does not mean that you should shower your code with trailing spaces or not use spaces at all. Take note that the right usage of spaces or white spaces in general can make your script easier to read.

## Physical Line and Logical Line

In programming, there are two types of code lines. The first one is physical line. The second one is logical line. A physical line is one line of code. It does not matter if it contains one or multiple statements. One row of code is equivalent to one physical line.

On the other hand, a logical line is one statement or valid line of code — usually, a statement terminator indicates the start and end of a logical line. In JavaScript's case, it is the semicolon symbol (;).

## Physical Line Length

To improve the readability of your code, it is best that you keep your physical lines' length to 80 to 120 characters long. Filling the entire length of your source code or text editor can make it difficult for you to read your source code.

A lengthy physical line can easily disorient your sight and location in the source code. Also, lines that exceed 120 to 160 characters can make text and source code editors enable the horizontal scroll bar, which is annoying.

On the other hand, it is recommended that you do not use the Word Wrap function of your code editor. It will make things look messier. And it might make you more prone to creating typos and syntax errors.

## Line Breaks

If it is unavoidable that one of your lines will exceed the recommended character length, you should take advantage of line breaks. For example, instead of doing this:

```
<script>
 var longString = "This is a very long text that you should break.";
</script>
```

Do it like this:

```
<script>
 var longString =
  "This is a very long text that you should break.";
</script>
```

However, make sure that you do it right. Do not place the line break in the middle of an enclosed value. If you do, you will get a syntax error. For example, doing it like this will produce an error:

```
<script>
 var longString = "This is a very long
  text that you should break.";
</script>
```

If you are confused on how to do it, just think of it as replacing a space. Instead of putting a space to separate the elements of your statement, use line breaks instead. For example, this is a valid way to break your physical line into multiple lines:

```
<script>
 var
 longString
 =
 "This is a very long text that you should break.";
</script>
```

> ***TIP***
> *Despite being a handy way to improve readability, try to think of other ways to make your physical lines short. Multiple methods exist to do that. Splitting your statements into multiple lines is not really pleasing to the eyes, too, and it can induce confusion and reduce the readability of your source code.*

## Case Sensitivity

Like a few programming languages, JavaScript is case-sensitive. Two words with different letter casings will be automatically considered as two different entities. For example, the keyword 'alert' will not work if you type it as 'ALERT.' If you try to do that in your page, you will receive an error like this:

Uncaught ReferenceError: ALERT is not defined

Because JavaScript or browsers treat 'alert' differently from 'ALERT' and you have not defined a variable, function, or any entity with the identifier 'ALERT,' you will receive an undefined error because the browser does not remember any existence of 'ALERT.'

## Camel Casing

If you have noticed in the previous examples, JavaScript tends to have 'words' that are typed in camel case (CaMeLCaSe/camelCase/CamelCase). For example:

document.getElementById("testImage").src = "/differentImage.jpg";

JavaScript has become like that because of the evolution in naming conventions in the program development industry. Back then, developers had three methods of dealing with variable or function names with multiple words.

First is the use of underscore:

> get_element_by_id

Second is the use of hypens:

> get-element-by-id

Third is the use of camel case:

> getElementById

These methods were devised since the character space is not useable in identifiers. The biggest reason JavaScript and most programming languages stick to camel case is that it is much more efficient. With the usage of underscore and dashes, additional keystroke for the dash and underscore is required when using variables with multiple words.

With camel case, they just need to press shift and the letter to capitalize. The capitalized letters were enough to distinguish that a name has multiple words in it. Also, dashes were not allowed in variable names, too, since dashes are often reserved to subtraction operations.

Also, camel-cased names in JavaScript always start with a small letter.

# Chapter 6: Statement and Its Parts

You might have seen the term 'statement' being used from time to time in the previous chapters. In programming, a statement is equivalent to a computer instruction. If compared to regular human language, a statement is an imperative sentence.

Just like regular sentences, a symbol is used to indicate when a statement is over. In the case of English sentences, it is a period (.). In the case of programming statements, it is a semicolon (;).

The semicolon is needed to be present in every statement to make sure that they will be separated from one another and not be considered continuous by the browser. Of course, exceptions exist.

For example, if a statement is not followed by another statement in the same line, the semicolon can be omitted. The line break between the two statements will serve as an indicator that they are two separate statements. Here is a sample:

<script>
 alert("Statement Number One")
 alert("Statement Number Two")
</script>

However, if you place the next statement in the same line with the first one, you will encounter an error, and the statements will not execute. For example:

```
<script>
 alert("Statement Number One")
alert("Statement Number Two")
</script>
```

In Google Chrome, you will receive an error like this for that:

Uncaught SyntaxError: Unexpected identifier

In Internet Explorer 8, you will receive an error like this instead:

Expected ';'

> ***NOTE***
> *Different browsers have different ways of handling JavaScript codes and errors. Due to that, it is essential that you adhere to coding standards and best practices. Even if it is okay to omit semicolons in most cases, it is still best to place them. Of course, this does not apply to semicolons only.*
>
> *You should do that to make sure that your code will work in all browsers. It also allows other people to understand and analyze your code easily. The same benefits go to you, too.*

***TIP***
*You can put multiple statements in one line in JavaScript. By separating them with semicolons, you will not have a problem. However, it is best to not do it so much. Most coding styles advise programmers to stick with one line (physical line) per statement. It reduces confusion and is easier on the eyes — though for short programs, it is not aesthetically pleasing.*

Just like regular English sentences, JavaScript statements also have small components within, too, that are put together to create a valid and coherent computer instruction. A few of those elements are:

- Literals
- Operators
- Variables
- Keywords
- Comments

## Literals

Literals can be referred to as data or values. They are the values you declare within your source code or values that have been evaluated from expressions and functions you created. A literal often represents a fixed value in your program.

In JavaScript, multiple types of literals exist. Some of them are:

- Integer: numerical values without the decimal point or fractional value. This type represents whole numbers. Integers in JavaScript can be shown in three forms or conversions: decimal (base 10), hexadecimal (base 16), and octal (base 8).
- Floating: numerical values with fractional components and even imaginary numbers. Floating numbers can be expressed in scientific notation by including e or E to act as an exponent indicator.
- String: These are combinations of alphanumeric characters and/or symbols that are enclosed within single (') or double (") quotation marks. Strings are often used as text.
- Boolean: It has two values: true and false. Aside from numbers and text, computer programs deal with logical or truth values. They are commonly used in logical and comparison operations, which will be discussed later.
- Arrays: literals that can contain multiple literals within it. They can be accessed using indexes that you will set. And this will be discussed later.
- Objects: similar to arrays. If you have a programming background on an OOP (Object Oriented Programming) language, then you might get confused with this part, especially if you try to set arrays and objects apart in JavaScript. Nevertheless, you can assign pair values

in an object literal. This will be discussed later fundamentally.

## Variables

Literals are considered fixed values in programming. However, a normal program does not run on fixed values alone. Most of the time, it runs on variable values. In JavaScript or any programming languages, variable values are used and stored in variables.

Just like in mathematics, variables are 'symbols' (often as short as one letter) that represent a value — whether unknown or known. In programming, it works a bit differently, but don't worry — you will pick up how variables work easily.

Variables are no more than a container. They are just references to a certain value (changing or variable value). And they are handy in keeping track of those said values.

To create a variable, you must define it first. Here is an example:

<script>
 var exampleVariableJava;
 var x;
</script>


In the example, the script used the keyword or command **var** to tell the browser that it would define or create a variable in the page. In this case, the script created two variables: exampleVariableJava and x.

Of course, creating or defining a variable alone is not enough. It would be pointless to just create a value and not use it. To use a variable, you will need to assign values to it. To assign a value to a variable, you will need to use the assignment operator (=). For example:

```
<script>
 var exampleVariableJava;
 var x;
 exampleVariableJava = "This is a string.";
 x = 13;
</script>
```

With the use of the assignment operator, you will be able to assign any value or type of literal that you want in the variables you defined.

> ***TIP***
> *You can define and assign a variable in one statement. You can do that by using the **var** keyword first, follow it with the variable name that you want to use, the assignment operator, and then the value you wish to assign.*

***TIP***

*You can declare and assign values to multiple variables at once in one statement. All you need to do is this:*

*<script>*

*var q = 1, w = 2, e = 3;*

*</script>*

*In case that you do not want a long line, you can just break the declaration and assignment using line breaks. For example:*

*<script>*

*var q = 1,*

*w = 2,*

*e = 3;*

*</script>*

***TIP***

*It is best to place all of your variable declarations at the start of your script or code blocks. If you do that, it will be easy for you to check if you forgot to declare a variable. Also, it will prevent you from mixing the order of declaration and assignment of a value to the variable, which may result to an error.*

***NOTE***
*If you do not assign a value to a variable that you have defined, it will have the value of undefined. It is not a value per se, and it is more like the status or property of the variable that you have created.*

*Of course, you do not need to force yourself to put a value in every variable declaration that you make. Declaring variables without immediate value assignment is normal in programming.*

*That variable might store something that you need to calculate first or the user might input later.*

***NOTE***
*Redeclaring a variable will have no effect. It will not change the value of the variable and the variable will not be created or duplicated.*

## Identifiers

To create a variable, you must assign a 'name' for it. That name is called an identifier in programming. Identifiers are names. They must be unique.

Identifiers are assigned to variables, functions, and other elements in your program to make it easy for you to call, recall, invoke, and remember them. And since they should be unique, you cannot assign one identifier to multiple variables, functions, et cetera.

You must follow some rules to create an identifier. And if you do not follow those rules, you might receive a syntax error. Here are the rules when it comes to creating identifiers:

- Identifiers can be one letter long and there is no predefined limit on the maximum length of an identifier.
- Identifiers can be composed of dollar signs ($), underscores (_), letters, and digits.
- Identifiers can start with a letter, underscore (_), and a dollar sign ($), but never a number. This way, browsers will not be confused if an identifier is a number or an identifier for an element in your source code.
- Identifiers are case-sensitive. Variable x will be different from variable X.
- Keywords and reserved words cannot be used as identifiers. After all, they are identifiers that have been already used.

*TIP*

*You might already know or you might already have a style when it comes to naming variables, thanks to your experience in HTML and CSS. But for those who are totally new, it is essential that you establish a naming convention for your identifiers or variables.*

*The most common convention is to use a name that will describe the element that you will name. For example, if the variable will contain the name of the user, you might want to name it as userName or userFullName.*

## Operators

Of course, you would want to manipulate and do some operations in your program's fixed and variable values. In order to do that, you will need to use operators. In JavaScript, multiple types of operators exist. They offer different operations and results, and knowing each one of them will allow you to create complex operations and functions within your program.

But for now, you should start with the most common and familiar operators, which are arithmetic operators. Here are some examples:

```
<script>
 var f = 2 + 2;
 var g = 9 / 3;
 var h = 7 − 4;
 var i = 2 * 6;
</script>
```

***NOTE***
*Some operators behave differently according the data type of the literals or variables they are with. For example, using the addition (+) operator together will strings will make it behave as a concatenation operator. For example:*

*<script>*

*var f = "Philip";*

*var g = "Morris";*

*var h = f + g;*

*alert(h);*

*</script>*

*Since the addition operator was with strings, instead of performing an addition operation, it will combine or concatenate the strings. So, the value of variable h will become 'PhilipMorris'.*

# Assignment Operator

Of all the operators, the assignment operator deserves recognition. In any programming language, the assignment operator will be always the most used operator that you will utilize. By the way, when referring to the assignment operator, do not use equals, equal sign, or is equal to. In programming, equals has a different connotation. In JavaScript, equals refer to this operator: ==.

Also, it is worth mentioning that despite programming expressions and variable assignments being relatively similar to algebraic equations, assigning values to variables is completely different. For example, in algebra, x = x * 2 will lead you to confusion. Because first of all, how can a number (x) be equal to twice its current value (2x)? If you substitute a number to variable x, 7 for example, this is what will happen:

- x = x * 2
- 7 = 7 * 2
- 7 = 14

As you can see, that equation is faulty since 7 is clearly not equal to 14.

In programming, x = x * 2 means that you will assign or change the value of x to two times its previous value. If x's previous value is 6, x will be assigned a value of 12 since:

- x * 2 = 6 * 2 = 12

## Expressions

Expressions are combinations of literals, variables, operators, and/or keywords that force the computer to evaluate and return a value. A simple addition of numbers can be considered an expression.

And as you might have seen in the previous example, you can assign expressions to variables. However, do note that expressions get evaluated first, and then the resulting value of the evaluation will be the one that will be assigned to the variable. For example:

```
<script>
 var f = 2 + 2;
 var g = 9 / 3;
 var h = 7 - 4;
 var i = 2 * 6;
 alert(f);
 alert(g);
 alert(h);
 alert(i);
</script>
```

In the example, the script will create pop-up messages and provide you with the values that were assigned to the values. And if you tested it, you will see the values 4, 3, 3, and 12.

Just like in mathematics, you can use the variables in equations or expressions. The variable will provide the value of the literal it stores. For example:

```
<script>
 var x = 124;
 var y = 100 + x;
 alert(y);
</script>
```

In the example, the browser will end up providing you the number 224 since:

➢ y = 100 + x = 100 + 124 = 224

***NOTE***
*Including variables in expressions will not affect the value of the variable itself. Unless you used assignment operators (there are other assignment operators in JavaScript), the value of variables used in expressions will be unaffected during the evaluation.*

*Some other expressions or statements might affect the value of variable, but you do not need to worry about that yet.*

## Keywords

Keywords are special words that can perform specific commands and actions in your program. Keywords are built in to the language you are using. A few of the examples of keywords in JavaScript are **var** and **alert**.

Usually, keywords are placed or written as the first word in a statement. And because of that, it is easy to determine the action or command that a code will do.

JavaScript, just like any programming language, has a lot of keywords. Most of them will be mentioned, used, and explained along the way. As of now, the important thing that you should remember is that you cannot name your variables similar to keywords. After all, it is not okay to duplicate the use of an identifier.

For example, you cannot create a variable named **var** in JavaScript.

## Comments

In programming, coding can become confusing when your source code becomes huge. Since programming languages will force you to use similar words again and again, you can easily get lost in the sea of statements that you have created.

Because of that dilemma, programming languages have a built-in comment tag for you to write comments within your code. Comments are useful in multiple ways. What are comments anyway?

Comments are lines (some call them statements) that are ignored by compilers, interpreters, or in JavaScript's case, browsers. Comments are typically used as markers, explanations, statement disabler, and reminders.

And since statements are ignored by browsers, comment lines are unaffected by syntax. You can write whatever you want in comment lines or blocks. And because of that, writing explanations and reminders become easier.

Below are some examples on how you can use comments in your JavaScript code:

<script>
/* This is an example of a comment block.
Anything in between the comment opening tag
And the comment closing tag will be treated
As comments and will be ignored by browsers.
This is also the same as HTML comments. The
Only differences are that the opening and
Closing tags are different and you can only
Use these tags inside script tags.

On the other hand, most web and script developers
Use the first part of their script to provide
Information to the users or syndicators of their JavaScript code.

Aside from that, some uses comment blocks for

Long-winded explanations. */

```
// Start of the script.
// Declaration of variables goes in this section.
var x = "This is the first variable.";  // This line assigns a value
                    // to variable x
var y = "This is the second variable."; // Yes, you can put comments at
                    // the end of statements
// var x = "This is the third variable.";

// Since the above statement has a comment tag, it will not be read
// and executed by browsers.

// It is usual that most sample codes that you will find in books
// or the Internet take advantage of a single-line comment to
// explain stuff.

// On the other hand, commenting is a good method to disable
// some statements
// that you do not want to be executed temporarily.
// In most cases, it is considered good practice to comment out
// some of the lines that you want to delete.
// Since deleting a statement might make you regret doing so later,
```

// it will be best to keep them around for a while
// until you fully decide that they are useless and ready for deletion.
// Also, disabling statements with comments is a good way to
// use alternative statements without the fuss of deleting and retyping
// the previous or new statement.


// End variable declaration section.
// Other code goes here

</script>

As you can see, to create a comment, you will need to put two forward slashes (//) before your comment line. Comment lines are useful for one-line comments. Also, comment lines can be put at the end of statements. On the other hand, comment blocks are useful for long comments, manifestos, licensing information, and documentations. Of course, browsers will ignore all the comments in the example once they open the page.

## Chapter 7: Code Blocks and Functions

Truly, writing a program is just like writing a story in English. You have statements as your sentences. And like a normal sentence, a statement is composed of some essential parts and components. In this chapter, you will learn a level higher than a statement: code block.

A code block or block of code is like a paragraph. A code block is composed of statements that are enclosed within curly braces ({}). Typically, statements are grouped for a few particular reasons:

1. To allow browsers to execute them together since they need to be executed in a particular sequence to achieve a goal
2. To reduce the clutter in your source code
3. To create functions
4. To accommodate the syntax requirement of some keywords or statements

Primarily, code blocks are usually used because of reason number 3 and 4. In this section, you will be taught how to create a code block function.

## JavaScript Function

Creating JavaScript functions provide a lot of benefits to developers and their programs. A few of those reasons are:

1. To prevent automatic execution of statements
2. To be able to invoke or call a group of statements whenever or wherever in the script
3. To have a more organized code flow
4. To avoid redundancy in code

How can you create a function? To create one, you will need to use the function keyword. Creating a function is almost similar to declaring a variable. Below is an example:

<script>
 function thisIsMyFunction() { // code block starts with a curly brace
   // insert some statements here
   // for your code block
   // all the statements here will be executed
   // once the function is invoked or called
 } // the code block ends with a curly brace
</script>


In the example, the function keyword is used. The identifier thisIsMyFunction followed that, which names the function. Then, open and close parentheses were placed beside the function's name. Lastly, the code block followed.

You might be wondering about the purpose of the parentheses beside the function's name. Those parentheses are reserved for parameters, which will be discussed later. For now, copy the script below and try it on your browser:

```
<script>
 function threePopup() {
  alert("First Popup");
  alert("Second Popup");
  alert("Third Popup");
 }
</script>
```

Of course, create a proper HTML document and insert the script below. Once you are done, try opening the document. What happened? None, right? As mentioned a while ago, functions or code blocks are used to prevent the immediate execution of some statements. In this case, the three alert statements did not fire because it was enclosed inside a function.

# Invoking Functions in JavaScript

Take note that the code block or statements within a function will not execute as long as it is not invoked or called. So, how do you invoke a function anyway? It is easy. All you need to do is type in the function's name on the script. For example:

```
<script>
 function threePopup() {
  alert("First Popup");
  alert("Second Popup");
  alert("Third Popup");
 }

 threePopup();
</script>
```

Now, try running the page. This time, three pop-ups appeared, right? Invoking a function is as simple as that. However, as a reminder, do not forget the parentheses. If you do, the function will not be called.

## Alert

The keyword alert allows your script to create a pop-up box that will contain any message that you want. For the rest of the chapters, the alert box will be frequently used. This was discussed before, so this part will supplement some other information that was not mentioned.

Alert is also like a function. Unlike the functions you will create in your code, alert is already a predefined function in JavaScript. Alert is also a good example of a function that can take in arguments or value. And you can create a function like it, too, by adding parameters in your function.

## Function Parameters

Function parameters can allow your functions to take in values and use them inside the code block. Parameters are useful if your functions require values to be processed. Below is an example of code that replicates the alert keyword:

```
<script>
 function yourOwnAlert(message) {
  alert(message);
 }
 yourOwnAlert("This is the message");
</script>
```

Try running that script on your browser. As you can see, the function acted like it was like alert. It can take in values, and use it within the code block. As of now, do not worry about the actual statements behind alert — the sample was created that way to simplify things.

To add parameters, all you need is to provide identifiers for your parameters. Parameters can be used as variables. Once the function with parameters is called, all the arguments that will be passed on the invocation of the function will be assigned on the parameters. Then, the parameters can be used like variables within the code block.

A function can have none, at least one, or a lot of parameters in it. If you want to add more parameters, you can just add a comma separator and add another identifier that you wish to become a parameter. For example:

```
<script>
 function simpleAddition(operand1, operand2) {
  var operand3 = operand1 + operand2;
   alert("The sum of " + operand1 + " and " + operand2 + " is " + operand3);
 }
 simpleAddition(23, 56);
</script>
```

The example has the function simpleAddition and it can take two arguments for its two parameters: operand1 and operand2. When you run that script, you will receive a message that says, "The sum of 23 and 56 is 79".

# Chapter 8: Conditional Statements

There will be times that you will want your program or script to become adaptable to every situation. In some cases, you might want your script to react to any changes that might happen to the variables in your program.

Due to those possible scenarios, you will need to know how to take advantage of conditional statements. Conditional statements are like functions. Conditional statements have code blocks. However, instead of being called for the statements in the block to be executed, the program must satisfy the condition placed on it. Below is an example usage of a conditional statement:

```
<script>
 var variable1 = 2;
 if (variable1 > 3) {
   alert("The value of variable1 is greater than 3");
 }
</script>
```

## If Conditional Statement

The conditional statement if has three parts. The first is the if keyword. The next part is the condition that needs to be satisfied. And the last part is the code block that will be executed if the condition is satisfied.

In conditional statements, you will deal with comparison operators a lot. Comparison operators are operations that compare the operands that surround them. A few of JavaScript's comparison operators are: is greater than (>), is less than (<), is equal to (==), and is not equal to (!=).

In the previous example, the is more than comparison operator is used. When the browser evaluates a comparison operation, it will only return a Boolean value: true or false. The evaluation will return true if the comparison is correct. The evaluation will return false if the comparison is correct. In the example, the comparison was between variable1 and 3. This is how it will be evaluated:

- variable1 > 3
- 2 > 3
- Is 2 greater than 3?
- False

If variable1 is set to 4 or greater, this will happen:

- variable1 > 3
- 4 > 3
- Is 4 greater than 3?
- True

In case that the conditional or comparison check inside the parentheses of the if keyword returns true, its code block will be processed. If the check returns false, the code block will be ignored, and the browser will skip to the next statement after the code block.

In the example's case, since 2 > 3 = false, the code block will be ignored and the alert statement will not execute. If variable1 will be assigned with 4, the code block will be executed and the alert statement will trigger, which will result to a message box in the browser.

## If Else Conditional Statement

What if you want your program to do something else in case the if condition was satisfied? For example, what if you want to have an alert box pop-up in case that variable1 is less than 3? If you will rely on conditional statements alone, this will happen:

```
<script>
 var variable1 = 2;
 if (variable1 > 3) {
   alert("The value of variable1 is greater than 3");
 }
 if (variable1 < 3) {
   alert("The value of variable1 is less than 3");
 }

</script>
```

The above statement is good on its own. However, there is a much more efficient and faster way to pull off the same type of behavior. And that way is to use the else keyword. The else keyword is always used in conjunction with conditional statements. Below is an example on how to use else:

```
<script>
 var variable1 = 2;
 if (variable1 > 3) {
   alert("The value of variable1 is greater than 3");
 }
 else {
   alert("The value of variable1 is less than 3");
 }

</script>
```

Virtually, this example is equivalent to the previous one. The differences are:

> - The script used else instead of another if
> - The else statement did not have any conditional check

Else statements are always placed after a conditional statement. Its primary purpose is to execute a block code whenever the previous conditional statement was not satisfied. In this case, if the conditional check in the if statement returns false, the else statement will be satisfied and the browser will execute the statements in its block code.

If you test this example on your browser, you will see the message, "The value of variable1 is less than 3" because 2 is less than 1 — that is why the if statement received a false evaluation and the else statement got triggered.

## Else If Statement

What if variable1 was assigned a value of 3? If that happens, the script will not respond once it is executed. If you want the script to react to that, you will need to use an else if statement.

An else if statement is the combination of else and if. It will get triggered if the previous conditional statement was not satisfied and the condition on its if component is satisfied. Below is an improved version of the previous script:

```
<script>
 var variable1 = 3;
 if (variable1 > 3) {
   alert("The value of variable1 is greater than 3");
 }
 else if (variable1 == 3) {
   alert("The value of variable1 is equal to 3");

 {
 else {
   alert("The value of variable1 is less than 3");
 }

</script>
```

In this example, the following events will happen once you run it on your browser:

- Variable1 will have a value of 3.
- Check condition of if statement — is variable1 greater than 3?
- False — ignore code block of if statement.
- Move to next statement.
- Else if will be triggered since previous condition returned false.
- Browser will check the condition of else if.
- Is variable1 equal to 3?
- True — will execute code block of else if statement.
- Move to next statement.
- Else if will not be triggered since the previous conditional statement was satisfied.

## Applications

Conditional statements in JavaScript have a lot of applications. Two of the most common applications of conditional statements are:

- Creating checks for the client's user agent. You can check if the user is using a mobile phone or desktop computer to browse your website. Once you know what device he or she is using, you can use JavaScript to adjust the CSS settings of your site to accommodate the device your visitor is using.
- Checking if the user has properly filled up your website form. For example, you want to check if the user ticked a checkbox in your website form. If your visitor has not done that, you can make their browser inform them that they need to click the checkbox via a message box.

With just the if else conditional statements alone, you can create complex checks that can let you have full control of your web page. Another conditional statement exist in JavaScript, and that is switch, which you will learn in advanced lessons.

## Conclusion

Thank you again for purchasing this book!

I hope this book was able to help you learn about the fundamentals of JavaScript.

The next step is to apply what you have learned in this book.

Finally, if you enjoyed this book, please take the time to share your thoughts and post a review on Amazon. It'd be greatly appreciated!

Thank you and good luck!

# Preview of 'Python Programming For Beginners'

If you enjoyed JavaScript For Beginners you're sure to love this book!

# Chapter 1: Introduction to Python

If you typically work with computers, you will eventually find that there are certain tasks that you want to automate. For instance, you want to perform a search and replace over a huge amount of text files. You may also want to rearrange and rename a group of picture files in a complex manner. Perhaps, you would want to create a specialized graphical user interface (GUI) application, a computer game, or a custom database.

If you are a professional software developer, you may need to work with Java, C, or C++ libraries. However, you may find that the usual cycle for writing, compiling, testing, and re-compiling is too slow. Maybe you are creating a test suite for a library and think that writing the test code is tedious. Perhaps, you have created a program that can use an extension language and you do not want to implement and design an entire new language for the application.

If any of these cases apply to you, then Python is the perfect programming language for you. You can write Windows batch files or a UNIX shell script for your tasks. Just take note that shell scripts are most ideal for changing text data and moving around files. They are not ideal for games or GUI applications.

Python is easy to use and available on UNIX, Windows, and Mac OS X operating systems. It will allow you to quickly finish your tasks. It is a real programming language that offers much more support and structure for large programs than batch files and shell scripts. In addition, it offers much more error checking than C language.

Python is a high level language; therefore, it has built in high level data types, such as dictionaries and flexible arrays. It is also applicable to a bigger problem domain than Perl or Awk due to its general data types.

Through Python, you can split programs into modules for the purpose of reusing in other programs. It includes a vast collection of standard modules that you can use as reference. Some of these modules offer system calls, file I/O, sockets, and interfaces for GUI toolkits such as Tk.

Moreover, Python is an interpreted language that can save you so much time when you develop programs because linking and compilation are no longer necessary. You can use the interpreter interactively, making it easier to experiment with the features of the programming language. You will also find it easier to test functions and write throw-away programs. Python is also an efficient desk calculator.

Furthermore, Python allows programs to be written readably and compactly. Most of the programs created in Python are much shorter than Java, C, or C++. This is due to the following reasons:

- Statement grouping is performed by indentation rather than using brackets in the beginning and the end.

- The high level data types let you express complex operations in one statement.
- There are no argument or variable declarations required.

Python is actually extensible. So if you are knowledgeable in C language, it would be easy for you to add new modules or built-in functions to the interpreter. You would also be able to link programs to libraries, perform critical operations at high speeds, and link the interpreter to an application created in C and utilize it as a command language or extension for that particular application.

Python was developed by Guido van Rossum in the 1980's. Just like Perl, its source code is available under the GNU General Public License (GPL). It is case sensitive, which means that uppercase and lowercase characters require caution to be used. For instance, the words 'Harlequin', 'HARLEQUIN', and 'Harlequin' are all considered different terms.

And no, Python was not named after a reptile. It was, in fact, named after a television show called Monty Python's Flying Circus. References to the Monty Python skits in documentations are allowed and actually encouraged. How fun is that?

## Chapter 2: Learn The Basics

The syntax of Python is simple and straightforward. The language actually encourages programmers to create programs without the use of prepared or boilerplate code. The print directive is the simplest directive. It prints out a line and includes a newline.

Python has two major versions: Python 2 and Python 3. These two versions are different from each other. Python 2 is more common and more supported than Python 3, but the latter supports newer features and is more semantically correct.

The print statement is one notable difference between the two versions. In Python 2, it is not considered as a function, allowing it to be invoked without parentheses. In Python 3, however, it is considered as a function. Hence, it should be involved with parentheses.

## *Interactive Mode Programming*

Programs in Python can be executed in different modes of programming. When you invoke the interpreter without passing the script file as a parameter, you will obtain the following prompt:

```
$ python
Python 2.4.3 ( #1, Nov 11 2010, 13:34:43 )
[GCC 4.1.2 20080704 ( Red Hat 4.1.2 – 48 )] on linux2
Type "help", "copyright", "credits" or "license" for more information.
>>>
```

Once you see this prompt, you can type in the following text and press Enter:

```
>>> print "Hello Python World!";
```

If you are using a newer version, you have to use the print statement with parentheses:

```
>>> print ("Hello Python World!")
```

You will get the following output:

```
Hello Python World!
```

## *Script Mode Programming*

Using a script parameter to invoke the interpreter starts the execution and goes on until the script is done. Once the script is done, the interpreter no longer becomes active.

Take a look at the following sample program. It is written in a script and has the extension *.py*.

```
print "Hello Python World!";
```

If you type in the above source code in a test.py file and run it as

```
$ python test. py
```

you will get the following output:

```
Hello Python World!
```

Another way to execute scripts is to modify the *.py* file, such as:

```
#! /usr /bin /python
print "Hello Python World!";
```

If you run it as

```
$ chmod + x test.py
$ ./test.py
```

you get the following output:

```
Hello Python World!
```

### *Identifiers*

Identifiers are names used to identify variables, functions, classes, modules, and other objects. They start with an uppercase or lowercase letter. They may also start with an underscore ( _ ), followed by more letters or zero, as well as digits or underscores.

In Python, you cannot use punctuation characters, such as %, @, and $ within identifiers. Since it is case sensitive, you also have to be careful with your use of identifiers. Remember that *Example* and *example* are considered as two different identifiers because they are not exactly alike.

The following are the naming conventions for identifiers:

- The class names begin with uppercase letters. All other identifiers begin with lowercase letters.
- If an identifier ends with two trailing underscores, it is a language-defined special name.
- Identifiers that have only one leading underscore indicate that they are private.

- Identifiers that have two leading underscores indicate that they are strongly private.

## *Reserved Words*

The reserved words in Python are words that cannot be used as variables, constants, or any other identifier names. These keywords can only have lowercase letters. The following are the reserved words in Python:

| And | del | for | is | raise |
|---|---|---|---|---|
| Assert | elif | from | lambda | return |
| Break | else | global | Not | try |
| Class | except | if | or | while |
| Continue | exec | import | pass | with |
| def | finally | in | print | yield |

## *Indentation*

Indentation is a way to group statements. It is used for blocks in place of curly braces. The spaces and tabs are supported. However, standard indentation requires standard Python code to have four spaces. Consider the example as follows:

```
x = 1
if x == 1 :
    # indented four spaces
    print "x is 1."
```

## *Variables and Types*

As you have learned, Python is object oriented. It is not statically typed. Hence, there is no need for you to declare variables before you declare their type or use them. Each variable is an object.

### *Numbers*

Two types of numbers are supported in Python, and these are floating point numbers and integers. Complex numbers are also supported, though. Anyway, in order for you to define an integer, you have to use this syntax:

```
myint = 5
```

If you want to define a floating point number, can either use this notation:

```
myfloat = 5.0
```

or this one:

```
myfloat = float ( 5 )
```

Pick up your copy of 'Python Programing For Beginners' and continue your journey with the powerful and easy to learn Python programming.

Made in the USA
San Bernardino, CA
06 March 2018